BRINGING BACK THE
Mountain Gorilla

Ruth Daly

Crabtree Publishing Company
www.crabtreebooks.com

CRABTREE
PUBLISHING COMPANY
WWW.CRABTREEBOOKS.COM

Author: Ruth Daly

Series Research and Development: Reagan Miller

Picture Manager: Sophie Mortimer

Design Manager: Keith Davis

Editorial Director: Lindsey Lowe

Children's Publisher: Anne O'Daly

Editor: Ellen Rodger

Proofreader: Wendy Scavuzzo

Cover design: Margaret Amy Salter

**Production coordinator and
   Prepress technician:** Margaret Amy Salter

Print coordinator: Katherine Berti

Produced for Crabtree Publishing Company
by Brown Bear Books

Photographs
(t=top, b= bottom, l=left, r=right, c=center)

Front Cover: All images from Shutterstock

Interior: Alamy: Minden Pictures 8, Liam White 12; Getty Images: Howard Davies/Corbis 15t, Andrew Plumptre/Oxford Scientific 19t; iStock: Guenter Guni 23t, 26, USO 27b, VUS Limited 1; Nature Picture Library: Eric Baccega 25, Andy Rouse 20; Shutterstock: atm2003 22, Henk Bogaard 6, Brina L Bunt 10, Claire E Carter 7, Kiki Dohmeier 5b, Tetyana Dotsenko 16, 23b, Andrey Gudkov 5t, Karen Foley Photography 14, 17, Kit Korzun 27t, Mary Ann McDonald 4, Martin Mecnarowski 24, Vicki L Miller 29, Dmitry Pichugin 11, Damrong Rattanapong 28, Janos Rautonen 15b, LM Spencer 18, 19b, Russell Watkins 13.

Brown Bear Books has made every attempt to contact the copyright holder. If you have any information please contact licensing@ brownbearbooks.co.uk

Library and Archives Canada Cataloguing in Publication

Title: Bringing back the mountain gorilla / Ruth Daly.
Names: Daly, Ruth, 1962- author.
Series: Animals back from the brink.
Description: Series statement: Animals back from the brink | Includes index.
Identifiers: Canadiana (print) 20190128240 |
   Canadiana (ebook) 20190128259 |
   ISBN 9780778763147 (hardcover) |
   ISBN 9780778763260 (softcover) |
   ISBN 9781427123343 (HTML)
Subjects: LCSH: Mountain gorilla—Juvenile literature. |
   LCSH: Mountain gorilla—Conservation—Juvenile literature. |
   LCSH: Endangered species—Juvenile literature. |
   LCSH: Wildlife recovery—Juvenile literature.
Classification: LCC QL737.P94 D35 2019 | DDC j333.95/988416—dc23

Library of Congress Cataloging-in-Publication Data

Names: Daly, Ruth, 1962- author.
Title: Bringing back the mountain gorilla / Ruth Daly.
Description: New York, New York : Crabtree Publishing Company, [2020] | Series: Animals back from the brink | Includes index.
Identifiers: LCCN 2019023704 (print) | LCCN 2019023705 (ebook) |
   ISBN 9780778763147 (hardcover) |
   ISBN 9780778763260 (paperback) |
   ISBN 9781427123343 (ebook)
Subjects: LCSH: Mountain gorilla--Conservation--Africa, Central--Juvenile literature.
Classification: LCC QL737.P94 D35 2020 (print) |
   LCC QL737.P94 (ebook) | DDC 599.8840967--dc23
LC record available at https://lccn.loc.gov/2019023704
LC ebook record available at https://lccn.loc.gov/2019023705

Crabtree Publishing Company
www.crabtreebooks.com   1-800-387-7650

Printed in the U.S.A./082019/CG20190712

**Published in Canada
Crabtree Publishing**
616 Welland Ave.
St. Catharines, Ontario
L2M 5V6

**Published in the United States
Crabtree Publishing**
PMB 59051
350 Fifth Avenue, 59th Floor
New York, New York 10118

**Published in the United Kingdom
Crabtree Publishing**
Maritime House
Basin Road North, Hove
BN41 1WR

**Published in Australia
Crabtree Publishing**
Unit 3–5 Currumbin Court
Capalaba
QLD 4157

Contents

CRABTREE Plus

Find videos and extra material online at **crabtreeplus.com** to learn more about the conservation of animals and ecosystems. See page 30 in this book for the access code to this material.

Mountain Gorillas Under Threat

Mountain gorillas are large apes. They live in the wild in two areas of Central Africa. One **population** lives in the Bwindi Impenetrable National Park in Uganda. Another group lives in the Virunga National Park that borders Rwanda, Uganda, and the Democratic Republic of the Congo (DRC). Since mountain gorillas were discovered in 1902, their population has been steadily destroyed by **poaching**, disease, war, and **habitat** destruction. In 1971, only 254 mountain gorillas were thought to exist. In 1996, they were listed as critically **endangered**. By 2008, the population had risen slightly to around 680. In 2018, it was estimated that there were around 1,000 individuals and they were downlisted to endangered. But such low numbers of mountain gorillas remain a cause for concern.

Mountain gorillas live in groups of up to 30 individuals. These family groups are usually centered around one dominant, or most powerful, male called a silverback. When a male mountain gorilla is around 13 years old, the hair on his back turns silver, which is why they are called silverbacks.

GENTLE GIANTS

Mountain gorillas are herbivores, which means they eat leaves, stems, roots, and other types of vegetation. They rarely drink, as they get enough water from the plants they eat. Mountain gorillas are between 4 and 6 feet (1.2–1.8 m) tall when standing on their two back legs. They can weigh up to 440 pounds (200 kg) and eat up to 50 pounds (23 kg) of vegetation per day. A healthy gorilla can live for up to 54 years. Female gorillas are usually ready to breed by the age of 10, and give birth to a single baby about once every four to five years. When they reach adulthood, female gorillas leave the group they were born into and join a male gorilla in another group. Males are fully grown at about 15 years of age. They usually have to leave the group to start their own groups.

Currently, the mountain gorilla's habitat is limited to protected national parks, such as Volcanoes National Park in Rwanda.

Species at Risk

Created in 1984, the International Union for the **Conservation** of Nature (IUCN) protects wildlife, plants, and natural resources around the world. Its members include about 1,400 governments and nongovernmental organizations. The IUCN publishes the Red List of Threatened **Species** each year, which tells people how likely a plant or animal species is to become **extinct**. It began publishing the list in 1964.

The Western black rhino of Cameroon in Africa was last recorded by the IUCN in 2011. It is now classed as Extinct (EX). The IUCN updates the Red List twice a year to track the changing of species. Each individual species is reevaluated every five years.

SCIENTIFIC CRITERIA

The Red List, created by scientists, divides nearly 80,000 species of plants and animals into nine categories. Criteria for each category include the growth and **decline** of the population size of a species. They also include how many individuals within a species can breed, or have babies. In addition, scientists include information about the habitat of the species, such as its size and quality. These criteria allow scientists to figure out the probability of extinction facing the species.

IUCN LEVELS OF THREAT

The Red List uses nine categories to define the threat to a species.

Extinct (EX)	No living individuals survive
Extinct in the Wild (EW)	Species cannot be found in its natural habitat Exists only in **captivity**, in **cultivation**, or in an area that is not its natural habitat
Critically Endangered (CR)	At extremely high risk of becoming extinct in the wild
Endangered (EN)	At very high risk of extinction in the wild
Vulnerable (VU)	At high risk of extinction in the wild
Near Threatened (NT)	Likely to become threatened in the near future
Least Concern (LC)	Widespread, abundant, or at low risk
Data Deficient (DD)	Not enough data to make a judgment about the species
Not Evaluated (NE)	Not yet evaluated against the criteria

In the United States, the Endangered Species Act of 1973 was passed to protect species from possible extinction. It has its own criteria for classifying species, but they are similar to those of the IUCN. Canada introduced the Species at Risk Act in 2002. More than 530 species are protected under the act. The list of species is compiled by the Committee on the Status of Endangered Wildlife in Canada (COSEWIC).

GORILLAS AT RISK

The IUCN Red List classified mountain gorillas as Critically Endangered (CR) in 1996. Thanks to collaborative conservation efforts, the population had increased by 2008, but was still cause for great concern. In 2018, the Red List downlisted them to Endangered (EN).

Dangers of Human Contact

It is against the law to hunt mountain gorillas, but illegal poaching has contributed hugely to the threatened status of gorillas. As well as the deliberate killing of gorillas, hunters set **snares** made from rope or wire to trap antelope, buffalo, or small mammals. Young gorillas are often caught in these snares and are not able to free themselves. The wires wrap tightly around their limbs or fingers. Although park **rangers** may be able to rescue them, the gorillas are left seriously injured. If the rangers don't find them in time, the gorillas often die. There are also other dangers when humans and gorillas come into contact with each other. The common cold affects gorillas more severely than humans. It makes them seriously ill, or even kills them.

This silverback is missing a hand. It was caught in a snare. Poachers hunt mountain gorillas for their body parts, which are sold for use in traditional medicines, or as magic charms. High prices are also paid for the meat by illegal food traders.

A LOSING BATTLE

People living in the same area as the mountain gorillas use **charcoal** as a source of fuel for heating and cooking. Charcoal is made by burning wood from trees. Although it is now illegal to harvest charcoal in Virunga National Park, huge areas of forest have been cut down and destroyed. It is such a valuable industry that the illegal harvesting of charcoal continues in many places, destroying increasingly large areas of the gorillas' habitat. In the 1990s, violent conflicts between different groups of people forced thousands of people out of their homes. The refugees escaped to settle in the mountain forests. Illegal deforestation has since increased. Park rangers protecting the park and the gorillas are often attacked. Since 2009, 150 park rangers have been killed in Virunga as a result of unrest and conflict.

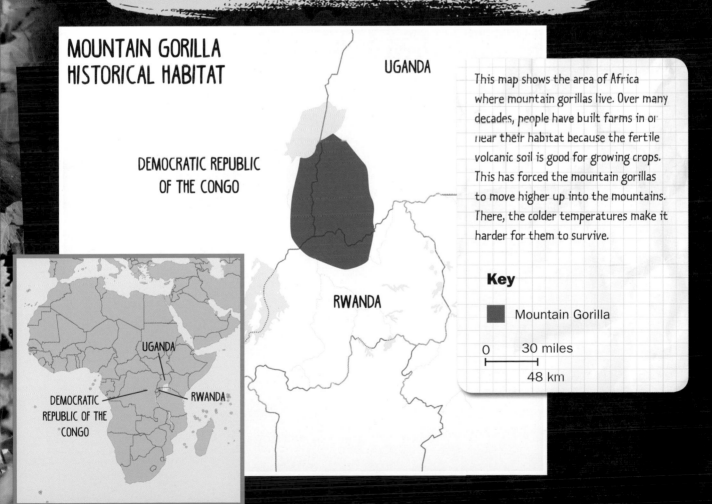

MOUNTAIN GORILLA HISTORICAL HABITAT

UGANDA

DEMOCRATIC REPUBLIC OF THE CONGO

RWANDA

UGANDA

DEMOCRATIC REPUBLIC OF THE CONGO

RWANDA

This map shows the area of Africa where mountain gorillas live. Over many decades, people have built farms in or near their habitat because the fertile volcanic soil is good for growing crops. This has forced the mountain gorillas to move higher up into the mountains. There, the colder temperatures make it harder for them to survive.

Key

Mountain Gorilla

0   30 miles
     48 km

Life in the Cloud Forests

The Virunga National Park has many habitats, including swamps, lava plains, steppes, and a chain of active volcanoes. In 1979, it was declared a UNESCO World Heritage Site. A wide variety of animals live in the park, including golden monkeys, hippos, leopards, and okapis. The bamboo forests high in the mountains are called **cloud forests** because they are covered in low cloud most of the time. This is where mountain gorillas live, at an altitude of between 8,000 and 13,000 feet (2,440 and 3,960 meters). Their other habitat, in Bwindi Impenetrable National Park, includes rain forest and **montane forest**. It is home to many species of birds and butterflies.

The high mountains of the Virunga National Park are often cloudy, misty, and cold. A day in the life of a mountain gorilla usually starts at dawn, when it begins to look for food. Just before dusk, the gorillas build themselves safe nests for the night using branches and foliage.

GORILLAS AND THE ECOSYSTEM

Mountain gorillas help to spread seeds from the plants they eat. These germinate and grow into trees, keeping the **ecosystem** healthy. Fruit only makes up about two percent of their **diet**. Although they like fruit, it is hard to find at high altitudes because of the cold climate. In the Virunga Mountains, gorillas feed on more than 100 different types of plants, including bamboo, wild celery, and thistles. Mountain gorillas are **grazers**, which means they do not destroy the whole plant when they are eating it. This helps it to grow back more easily, giving them more food to eat. Although they are mostly plant eaters, mountain gorillas also help the ecosystem by keeping ants, termites, and other pests under control. Apart from humans, the only **predators** of mountain gorillas are leopards, which occasionally attack young gorillas.

Baby gorillas drink their mother's milk for the first five months of their life. After that, they also start to eat stems and leaves. They are fully weaned from the mother's milk by the time they are about six years old.

Who Got Involved?

Conserving, protecting, and studying mountain gorillas are the main goals of the Dian Fossey Gorilla Fund International. Dr. Dian Fossey founded the **research** center in the Virunga Mountains in 1967. At that time, the park rangers were poorly trained and equipped, and poaching was increasing. Fossey spent many years living close to gorillas and observing their behavior in groups and individually. Gradually, the gorillas became **habituated**, which means they were used to her being around them. Part of Fossey's work became the education of the local people.

Dian Fossey was an American zoologist. She set up her research center in two small tents at Karisoke in 1967. Fossey was killed in Rwanda in 1985, but by then the center was internationally famous. Teams of scientists continued to work to protect the gorillas in Virunga National Park.

GORILLA DOCTORS

In 1984, Fossey asked the Morris Animal Foundation, a group funding animal health projects around the world, for help providing veterinary care to wild gorillas in Rwanda. Dr. James Foster arrived in 1986, serving as the first "Gorilla Doctor." Originally called the Mountain Gorilla Veterinary Project, Gorilla Doctors help sick and injured gorillas in the forest. Observing and **monitoring** wild gorillas regularly is necessary for the project to be effective. Today, the program includes other gorilla species, orphaned gorillas, and health care for people living in or near gorilla habitats.

COLLABORATING FOR A CAUSE

The World Wildlife Fund (WWF) was founded in 1961 to help protect endangered species around the world. Since then, the organization has worked to stop poaching and **logging** in gorilla habitats by providing food and homes for local people. The WWF is also part of another group called the International Gorilla Conservation Programme (IGCP), which works with Flora & Fauna International. They work with local conservation groups and park authorities based in Rwanda, Uganda, and the DRC to protect the mountain gorilla habitat. The IGCP is also involved in taking a **census** of mountain gorilla **troops** on a regular basis to monitor their numbers and keep track of their health and movements.

Raising Awareness

The Dian Fossey Gorilla Fund worked with local governments and groups in the communities close to gorilla habitats. It also collaborated with other international organizations. Research to increase awareness and understanding of mountain gorillas worldwide was a key part of the plan. Helping people solve their problems had a direct impact on saving gorillas. During the war in Rwanda between 1990–1994, many **refugees** escaped to the mountains hoping to find safety, shelter, and food. To survive, they used trees for firewood and hunted gorillas for food. The World Wildlife Fund knew that they would need to help the people in order to protect the gorillas and their habitat.

Dian Fossey believed in "active conservation." She removed traps and confronted poachers. Her favorite gorilla, Digit, was killed in 1977. After that, she began a campaign to raise public awareness. In 1983, she wrote *Gorillas in the Mist*. The book was turned into a successful movie in 1988.

Refugees had to leave their homes during the Rwandan Civil War (1990–1994). This was a bloody conflict between the government's army and rebels.

WORKING TOGETHER

The habitat of mountain gorillas includes land in three different countries: Rwanda, the DRC, and Uganda. This presented early conservationists with a problem. At that time, each country had different laws and approaches to dealing with their gorilla populations. An important role of the IGCP was to help various groups based in those countries work together. They developed policies to protect the forests, resources, and wildlife that crossed their borders, which included the protection of mountain gorillas.

Tracking the Gorillas

Teams of trackers have an important job to do. They watch and monitor the mountain gorilla population. They find groups of gorillas by following the signs left behind as they move through the forest. Gorillas build new nests each night, then move on looking for food. What they leave behind—broken vegetation, hand prints, discarded food—gives trackers information. When the gorillas have been found, the teams note the health and appearance of each individual gorilla. They also notice if any gorillas are missing from the troop, and make a record of any births and deaths. The information is shared with governments and conservation groups. Tracker teams also play an important role in keeping gorillas safe because they are able to help any that have been trapped and left behind in snares.

A ranger and a tracker in Volcanoes National Park follow the trail of a troop of mountain gorillas. The foliage has been disturbed where the gorillas have passed through the jungle.

CHALLENGES TO RECOVERY

In the 1990s, the WWF began working with the United Nations, another international organization. They provided the Rwandan refugees with alternative fuel supplies to save the trees from being cut down for firewood. However, by 2004, more than 3,706 acres (1,500 ha) of mountain gorilla habitat had been destroyed. Refugees from the DRC and Rwanda built illegal settlements and cleared the land for crops and livestock. The WWF funded **reforestation** programs to replace trees in some of these areas. It also worked with local people to provide education about their environment. This helped them to manage the natural resources in ways that would be less harmful to the environment. The WWF continues to work with governments and timber companies to encourage more environmentally friendly practices.

A mountain gorilla community awareness training day held in Bwindi Impenetrable National Park, Uganda.

COLLABORATING FOR A CAUSE

The new Ellen DeGeneres campus of the Dian Fossey Gorilla Fund International is scheduled to open in 2021. The campus will provide a permanent base for education and research, and will have laboratories, classrooms, offices, a library, and exhibits about the work of Dr. Fossey. The local economy has benefited during the construction of the campus, with the creation of jobs for local people and the use of nearby resources.

Protecting the Gorillas

The IGCP met regularly with people from different interest groups to explain the need for conservation. Farmers and environmental experts met with representatives from the national parks, military, and governments to find ways they could work together. Ranger-based **patrols** were introduced to monitor the movements of gorillas, and to report on any poachers or other signs of human activity in the area. Information was shared between Rwanda, Uganda, and the DRC. This helped rangers to respond when poaching and illegal logging took place, or when gorillas were in danger. In 2001, the IGCP was assigned to help the three countries create a protected area of land.

A ranger patrols Virunga National Park, DRC, in 2015. He is armed with a radio and an AK-47 assault rifle. There are around 400 rangers. Protecting gorillas is one of the most dangerous jobs in the world.

COLLABORATING FOR A CAUSE

Veterinarians from Gorilla Doctors work with local trackers to check for signs of illness in mountain gorilla troops. If they spot any weak gorillas that are coughing and sneezing, vets treat them using antibiotics. Dull or patchy hair is another sign of illness. Rescuing gorillas from snares involves a team of vets, park staff, trackers, and porters. This can be a tricky process because other members of the gorilla troop are often watching nearby. A dart containing anesthetic is used to **tranquilize** the trapped gorilla. Once it has been freed, the gorilla is treated with antibiotics. It can usually be returned to the troop immediately.

Many gorillas are orphaned in human attacks. Poachers often kill adult gorillas to capture a young gorilla alive. They sell them as pets. The Gorilla Doctors look after rescued orphans. They look after their mental and physical wounds. Some are returned to the wild. Others would not survive in the wild. They are sent to sanctuaries.

Back from the Brink?

The gorilla populations in Bwindi Impenetrable National Park and Virunga National Park slowly began to increase. In 2018, the total population was at least 1,000. Strict anti-poaching laws, the removal of snares, and the provision of medical care for sick and injured gorillas had all begun to take effect. However, snares remain a threat. In 2018, Gorilla Doctors removed snares from Rwanda, Uganda, and the DRC. Around 1,000 snares are found in Rwanda each year. In the last 10 years, 24 mountain gorillas were trapped. In 2014, Prosper Uwingeli, the Chief Park Warden of the Rwandan section of Volcanoes National Park, launched a campaign aimed at educating local people. They learned how money gained from gorilla tourism could be used to help their own communities. As a result, several former poachers helped to find and destroy gorilla snares.

Local people set snares and traps by tying a noose of rope or wire to a branch or bamboo stem. The branch is then pulled downward, bending it. A stick or rock is used to hold the branch down. When an animal steps into the noose, the branch springs up, pulling the animal up into the air.

REDUCING POVERTY HELPS GORILLAS

Many people living in or near the mountain gorillas' habitat were living in **poverty**. Some were surviving on less than $2 a day. They depended on farming to support their families. This meant clearing the forests so they could grow crops. The IGCP helped farmers to find other ways to earn a living. They encouraged them to become guides, or to make handicrafts to sell to tourists. If farmers did not want to give up their farms, the IGCP taught them to farm without using pesticides, and to plant organic seeds such as garlic to improve the soil. The IGCP also gave the farmers financial help if gorillas strayed onto the farms and damaged the crops. People began to understand that protecting the environment helped everyone, including gorillas.

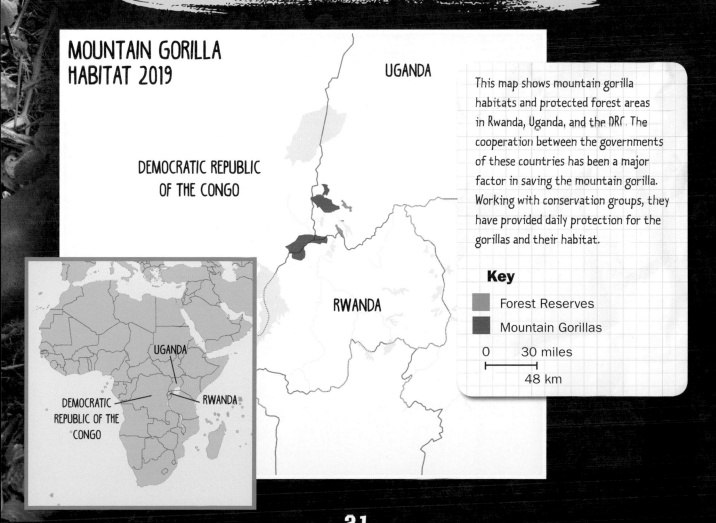

MOUNTAIN GORILLA HABITAT 2019

UGANDA

DEMOCRATIC REPUBLIC OF THE CONGO

RWANDA

This map shows mountain gorilla habitats and protected forest areas in Rwanda, Uganda, and the DRC. The cooperation between the governments of these countries has been a major factor in saving the mountain gorilla. Working with conservation groups, they have provided daily protection for the gorillas and their habitat.

Key

Forest Reserves

Mountain Gorillas

0   30 miles

48 km

UGANDA

DEMOCRATIC REPUBLIC OF THE CONGO

RWANDA

Gorilla Tourism: Good or Bad?

Conservation groups encourage tourists to visit mountain gorillas. Local communities, as well as conservation groups, benefit from tourism. Jobs are created for local people who work in hotels and restaurants, make and sell souvenirs, and work as gorilla guides. Between 2006 and 2013, about $75 million was gained via tourists visiting the mountain gorillas. Some of that money was used to fund more than 300 community projects. In Rwanda, 57 primary schools and 12 health clinics were built, improving the quality of life for approximately 40,000 local people.

The Batwa tribe from Uganda are known as "conservation refugees." For thousands of years, they lived in the same forests as mountain gorillas. They did not hunt or harm them. When the national parks were created, the government forced the Batwa off their lands. They now make a small living as tour guides, and by performing the traditional Intore dance for tourists.

WHAT'S THE DOWNSIDE?

Mountain gorillas live in small groups. Any illness can quickly spread. If too many gorillas die, the troop may not be able to survive. Tourists who are sick, even with a minor cold, are not allowed into protected areas. All visitors are also told to keep at least 22 feet (7 meters) away from gorillas. This includes times when the animals might wander out of protected areas toward the tourist lodges. The construction of roads, hotels, and other buildings necessary for large numbers of tourists can sometimes also destroy parts of the mountain gorillas' habitat.

Souvenirs are big business in Virunga National Park. Alongside traditional crafts, tourists can buy T-shirts featuring the names and images of the various mountain gorilla troops.

Looking to the Future

The main threat to the future of mountain gorillas comes from people. Although the gorillas live in remote areas, about 100,000 people now live there too. The number of people greatly increases the chances of diseases being passed to the gorillas. Protecting the habitat is another important factor in the survival of the species. The recent discovery of oil in Bwindi Impenetrable National Park has caused concern. The government of the DRC has removed around 21.5 percent of the national park from protection, prioritizing oil production over conservation. It is feared that the decision will damage tourism and further endanger the lives of gorillas and rangers. Oil drilling is also expected to release large amounts of carbon dioxide into the air, increasing the rate of **climate change**.

Conservationists have been able to slow the spread of habitat destruction. This view of the border of Virunga National Park clearly shows where the forest has been cleared for farming. Trees remain in the protected area on the other side of the border. If more can be done to make the forests safe for mountain gorillas and visitors, gorilla populations will increase.

Orphanage centers help to save mountain gorillas and keep the population growing. Here, a keeper plays with a young female at the orphanage center in Rumangabo, in the DRC area of the Virunga National Park.

DANGERS IN THE FOREST

Although there has been progress in reducing poaching, snares continue to injure and kill mountain gorillas. Having the money to fund daily patrols remains vitally important. Governments and conservation groups continue to work to prevent fighting between armed groups hiding in the forests. The park was closed for several months between 2018 and 2019, when it became too dangerous for rangers and tourists to travel within the park. When the park is closed, tourism is affected and local communities suffer financially. Future changes in climate could shrink the mountain gorilla habitat further and reduce their food sources. However, mountain gorillas are able to survive in a wide range of temperatures and also have a varied diet. Some scientists think climate change will not affect mountain gorillas as badly as some other species.

Saving Other Species

Lessons learned in the fight to save the mountain gorillas are being used to protect other endangered gorilla species and **subspecies**. Many of the same organizations are involved, including the WWF, Gorilla Doctors, and the Dian Fossey Gorilla Fund International. The threats faced by all gorilla species are similar, so it is possible that many of the methods used to help the mountain gorilla will prove equally successful. The eastern lowland gorilla, also known as Grauer's gorilla, is found only in the tropical rainforest lowlands of the DRC. Fighting in the region has made an accurate count difficult. Poaching, habitat destruction, and human activity, including mining, are consistent threats to their survival.

The population of the eastern lowland gorillas has fallen steadily since the mid–1990s, when it numbered around 17,000 individuals. Today, the population is around 4,000 or less. The IUCN lists it as Critically Endangered.

THE LAST FEW HUNDRED

The Cross River gorilla is the rarest of all apes. It is estimated that there are 200 to 300 of these gorillas left in the wild. An accurate count is difficult because these apes are not habituated, or used to people, and they live in rugged forest habitat in Nigeria and Cameroon. One of the main threats is logging, for timber and to clear land for farming. This has led to habitat loss. Poaching is also a threat. The status of the Cross River gorilla is currently listed by the IUCN as Critically Endangered.

INTO SIX FIGURES

The western lowland gorilla lives in several countries in West Africa. It lives mainly in remote forests and swamps, which makes an accurate count difficult. The total population is thought to number around 100,000 individuals, giving it the highest population of all gorilla species. Poaching for **bushmeat** was one reason for their decline, along with habitat loss due to the mining industry and oil palm plantations. Diseases such as the Ebola virus have also harmed the population. This gorilla also remains Critically Endangered on the IUCN Red List.

Mountain Gorillas Need You!

The mountain gorilla is back from the brink of extinction, but it is far from safe. Saving gorillas takes commitment from everyone. One way you can help is to recycle your cell phones, laptops, and other electronic equipment. If everyone did that, it would reduce the demand for metals and minerals that are being mined in Virunga National Park. Find out which organizations or businesses in your community recycle cell phones and other electronics. You could organize a community project to collect old electronic equipment for recycling.

Take good care of the electronics you currently have so they don't need to be replaced so often. When buying a new phone, camera, or computer, ask yourself if it is something you really need. Perhaps you could give the money you save to the gorilla fund instead!

Raising funds is one of the best ways you can help to protect the mountain gorillas. These people are taking part in the Denver Gorilla Run to raise funds for the Mountain Gorilla Conservation Fund in Africa.

SPREAD THE WORD

You may not be able to travel to see the mountain gorillas, but you can learn more about them. Spreading information and educating people is a great way to help. Here are some ideas you can try:

- Prepare a PowerPoint presentation for your class about the work of one of the conservation groups featured in this book. Explain how the group helps mountain gorillas. Contact one of the conservation groups to see how else you might be able to help.

- Habituated mountain gorillas in Rwanda are given names in an annual naming ceremony called Kwita Izina. Organize a "Save the Mountain Gorilla" day. Ask people to enter a draw to give a name to a toy gorilla. Give the money you raise to the gorilla fund.

- Write your elected representative or local newspaper explaining why you feel strongly about saving mountain gorillas. Urge them to support some of the international conservation groups.

Learning More

Books

Dakers, Diane. *Dian Fossey: Animal Rights Activist and Protector of Mountain Gorillas*. Crabtree Publishing, 2016.

Doak, Robin S. *Dian Fossey: Friend to Africa's Gorillas* (Women in Conservation). Heinemann, 2014.

Hirsch, Rebecca E. *Mountain Gorillas: Powerful Forest Mammals* (Comparing Animal Traits). Lerner, 2017.

McDowell, Pamela. *Gorillas* (Amazing Primates). Av2 by Weigl, 2016.

On the Web

www.animalplanet.com/wild-animals/endangered-species/mountain-gorilla/
Learn some cool facts about mountain gorillas and watch a short video of a troop in the mountains.

vimeo.com/191794005
Sir David Attenborough has made many well-known documentaries about nature. Watch him interact with mountain gorillas in Rwanda during his visit there in the 1970s. From the series *Life on Earth*.

www.youtube.com/watch?v=EUvwvmm7oL4
Watch an interview with two veterinarians who work for the organization, Gorilla Doctors. Learn about their work and hear some of the sounds that mountain gorillas make!

www.youtube.com/watch?v=LaxWCxseYZk
Watch this short video made by Grade 5 students in Canada about what action they took to help mountain gorillas.

CRABTREE Plus

For videos, activities, and more, enter the access code at the Crabtree Plus website below.

www.crabtreeplus.com/animals-back-brink

Access code: abb37

Glossary

bushmeat Meat from African wild animals that is used for food

census A count of the population

charcoal A type of black solid ash left when wood is burned. It can be used as fuel

climate change A change in normal global weather patterns

cloud forest Forests at high altitudes, frequently covered by clouds

conservation The preserving and protecting of plants, animals, and natural resources

decline To fall in number

diet The range of food eaten by a type of animal

ecosystem Everything that exists in a particular environment, including animals and plants, and nonliving things, such as soil and sunlight

endangered In danger of becoming extinct

extinct Describes a situation in which all members of a species have died, so the species no longer exists

grazers Animals that eat small amounts of vegetation throughout the day

habitat The natural surroundings in which an animal or plant lives

habituated When animals are comfortable being around humans

logging Cutting down trees for wood

monitoring To observe something closely and record information

montane forests Forests above an altitude of 1,640 feet (500 m)

patrols Keeping watch on an area

poaching Illegal hunting

population The number of people, animals, plants, etc., living in an area at an exact time

poverty Not having enough money for basic needs

predators Animals that kill and eat other animals

rangers People who patrol an area

reforestation Replanting of an area where vegetation has been removed

refugees People who flee their homeland because of conflict

research To study and gather information about a subject

snares Devices used to trap animals

species A group of similar animals or plants that can breed with one another

subspecies A species within a group, but which has different or new features

tranquilize To make an animal quiet and relaxed with a drug

troops The name given to families of gorillas

Index and About the Author

ABOUT THE AUTHOR
Ruth Daly has more than 25 years of teaching experience, mainly in elementary schools, and she currently teaches Grade 3. She has written more than 45 nonfiction books for the education market on a wide range of subjects and for a variety of age groups. These include books on animals, life cycles, and the natural environment. Her fiction and poetry have been published in magazines and literary journals. She enjoys travel, reading, and photography, particularly of nature and wildlife.